Elephant Wisdom:

Poetry on Science, Religion, Division, & Loss

M. Gail Grant

Keebie
Press
PO Box 5315
Canton, GA 30114

ISBN-13: 978-1-7358875-2-4

Dedication

This book is dedicated to every child, young and old alike, that still embraces a sense of wonder through curious exploration, not hesitating to question the status quo. In other words, anyone that embraces the elephant in the room, willing to talk about life's difficult moments, mysterious idiosyncrasies, and societal principles, seeking support from those eager to listen with their soul.

Table of Contents

Part I:

Part II:

Part I:

Science, Religion, and Division

Collective Consciousness,

Parapsychology, Astronomy,

Physics, Persuasion,

&

God

Awareness

Numbness surrounds us all each and every day,

and we don't even realize

the profoundness that is interwoven

in the essence of our lives.

From birth to death,

there is a supernatural element

hiding in the shadows, guiding us

through each moment in time —

a time that doesn't really exist

but an imaginary

measurement that governs

our spiritual journey.

Humanity has the ability to

embrace the elements of life

that makes sense, and to

tuck inconsistencies away

in small corners of the brain,

for the truth before us

is sometimes just too complicated

to understand.

Great scientists of the past

used simple instruments to confirm

that both time and space bend in the

heavenly space above sweet earth.

What does this mean,

you may ask,

for all that it's worth

is a line of prose

in scholarly textbooks.

The connection of

knowledge and spirituality

is broken at best,

for many of us arise each morning

with no thought of the rest,

just to robotically move forward

each minute of 'time'

until our pilgrimages on this

  planet abruptly unwind.

Maybe one day,

a unification will occur

with a marriage between

scientific study on the fabric of our universe

and the one who governs the stars.

Perhaps, science and religion

will one day concur

that joining forces may just be

the answer in solving the mysteries

behind each frequency of life,

for each Sunday when I sit in the church,

I am reminded

of how great life

is beyond the boundaries of the earth,

or as I sit in

the collegiate classroom in such awe,

learning about heavenly bodies —

how their will governs us all.

Sitting on the beach,

and darkness takes over,

the salty tide begins to rush the

sand beneath my feet,

as the water slowly creeps into

my personal space,

reminding me of the moon

and its powerful presence,

changing ocean tides with a magnificence

beyond human existence.

Yet, somehow,

in the strangeness of it all,

the idea is smothered,

bringing the everyday reality back

as I begin to softly dread

work tomorrow.

Hidden Dimensions

What if heaven is closer than we think?

When the body dies, the vacancy of spirit is
apparent to the human eye. Although,
optics within the visual spectrum may
be misleading to universal truth.

The mind manifests a vast distance
between heaven and earth,
but what if the awareness of reality is just that —
nothing more than human perception —
a hologram, perhaps?

While grief from the loss
of a loved one can be encompassing,
many stories are told
of spiritual visitations.

Sensual appearances bequeathing
hair-raised arms, familiar scents, and inexplicable
synchronicities
clog 'underground' blog posts,
yet science seems to avoid
the 'para' unknown.

From shamans
to ancient witch doctors,
historical accounts of interactions
with the vast unknown
seem to find their way to those grasping
for a sense of connection
beyond earthly parameters.

The truth is no one knows
because as long as science cannot
prove the existence of obscure
dimensions in space and time,
mainstream outlets will not embrace
the possibility of another lifeform
that interacts with this world of ours.

Discrediting, debunking,
and demoralizing
humanity's sixth sense,
the one that unifies us to the field
of connected consciousness,
is a means of mass control.

Religion, as a whole,
is a teaching that calls
on faith and fear

to guide our every move
for the benefit of those in power,
but it begins to break down
and disintegrate into dust
when used as a technique
to merely visit our ethereal home.

Could it be intertwined
in our DNA
that the essence of our nature
knows how to journey
between the hidden dimensions
within this thing called space?

As slaves
to the prescribed messages,
we live,
denying the existence
of a presence,
such as His.

The soft whispers that wake us
from a deep sleep
in the middle of the night
may just be
His way of saying

'awaken my child,'
for the mysteries that plague this world
are underneath
a blanket laden with money and sin
by men who thirst
for the grandest of things –
money, power, and status
from pledging allegiance
to the most profound secrets
that lay within
wickedness.

When the world feels dark,
and the mind begins to question
the normalcy of it all,
remember the most fundamental ingredients
of faith
are to quietly spend time with Him,
rejecting the doctrines of serpents disguised as men,
for what lies within the soul
has yet to be explained in an earthly sense.

Forgive often,
embrace love over hate,
quiet the mind,
and let the soul emanate

mother earth's sweet breath
bundled inside invisible waves.

Childlike Notions

Children see more without their eyes than adults do throughout their lifetime.

This is an untapped field of knowledge by means of collective consciousness that goes unnoticed.

At young ages, children have not yet been trained to ignore their sixth sense — their body's ability to cohesively connect the body and the soul.

I wonder what the world would be like without operant conditioning.

Dark Energy

I remember reading in a collegiate cosmology textbook that 93% of the universe is classified as "unknown," suggesting a composition of what scientists have coined dark matter and dark energy.

Could this be "God?"

It seems like humanity only understands approximately 7% of life. Maybe the percentages have changed, but the sentiment is the same.

We have no idea.

Starlight Embrace

His death eroded her soul — the vastness of the infinite heavens, a constant reminder of his absence.

Educated in cosmology, she knew the starlight above represented brilliance that had left its source millions of years ago. The irony was too much to fathom. Gone too soon, yet still so close, or maybe not; the universe was nothing but a mirage.

Transcending parallel universes, traveling across bent dimensions of time and space, was something she never thought possible. *Why not?* She wondered.

Closing her eyes, focusing her breathing, relaxing her mind, she felt the breeze whip through her hair as bodily sensations of flight took over. *Could this be what others had experienced?*

Speed increased, her ears detected a gentle hum, the air temperature became colder. Star luminosity and rhythmic cadence seemed to bring forth unrealized calmness and internal peace. Enormous clouds of dust danced in the night sky, showcasing an array of infinite colors she could not quite recognize.

Time stood still. She felt his embrace. No words were spoken. His presence was definitive yet as gentle as a baby's breath.

Her eyes opened.

The moment was gone but never to be forgotten — their dance among heavenly stars.

Stargazer

Have you ever noticed how humans naturally look to the stars when they feel lost?

It seems there is an internal coding, if you will, that teaches us when our lives are in such disarray, and we don't know where to turn, that we should simply 'look up' for guidance and direction.

Stargazing is a favorite pastime of mine, and it took me years to realize the 'why' behind such coveted moments of the designated time.

For, you see, it could be that the soul remembers where it came from and hopes to eternally be journeying home once the seeds of lessons during earthly life have been sewn.

A Bluebird's Melody

That feeling that something or
someone is looking over your
shoulder comes from your
sixth sense.

Have you ever wondered why we
pretend that this feeling isn't real
or why we simply shrug it off as
our mind playing tricks on us?

Could it be that we have been
conditioned through external
forces to discredit our own
synergy with the universal bond?

What if each bluebird we see is a
gentle reminder that there are
love and life beyond the grave?

The bible says God breathed life
into Adam and Eve and that

returning to the dust of the earth
is how we will leave, yet science
tells us intricately woven stardust
is all that makes us beings.

Upon earthly death, the heart no
longer beats, and the spirit inside
tenderly escapes, leaving nothing
but stardust in the shallow grave.

Science has proven religion, and
it would seem that controversy
would end, and togetherness
bring about a connectedness
between all of humanity.

God's name is debated among
denominations of thought, but
the ultimate test is not what
He is called.

The importance lies in the
brotherhood of it all; joining
likeness with others is the
purpose of the fall.

Each time a bluebird visits,
remember its song,
as messages beyond this world
have traveled so far.

Astral Travel

What would happen

if the soul

decided to take

a vacation?

Would it carry a suitcase?

What would happen

to the human body

if our soul

needed a break?

Some claim

the ability to

spiritually travel

between multiple dimensions

of

time and space.

My soul traveled

for a few seconds,

just once.

The magnificence

of those moments

don't compare

to anything

experienced on this earth.

There are no words

in the English language

that can describe

the brilliance

of color, ambiance, and emotion

that occurred.

It almost seemed like

an experience

a baby may have

in its mother's womb,

tossing and turning

in an awestruck sight.

The opportunity

may never again arise,

but the lesson was learned.

Our soul knows how to journey back,

and somewhere in the stars above

is where our soul calls home.

Heaven's Nightlight

Stars shine

brightly at night,

illuminating all

mysteries of the great, vast sky

~ twinkle.

Synchronicities

When two minds learn

how to intertwine,

the result is cataclysmic.

Meditation submerges

the essence of the body

into a universal space

beyond the physical

restraints of earth.

Synchronicities occur

as a subtle

suggestion to the mind

that these small

gifts are meant

to remind

humanity

that the power

has always

lain within.

Energy is a lifeforce

that evades all space,

changing outcomes

on a whim

with the blessings

of those brave enough

to just look within.

Grow your mind,

and your soul will follow.

Conscious Reality

If thought creates reality, you made the mess.

If thought creates reality, you can change the situation.

If thought creates reality, your reality is a manifestation of how you really feel. It's like your mind is looking in a mirror, and the reflection becomes truth.

Mortal Purpose

As the essence of the soul

matures through the battles of earthly life,

guilt and remorse seem to always occur,

for knowledge is powerful

and leads to more calculated sunrises.

Bury the sadness

of the new awareness that arises,

for educating the soul is the

purpose

of this life.

The Wind

The wind is a force that cannot be controlled. Nothing exists that can deter the wind. Try as we must, science and technology can merely harvest the energy beneath its wings.

As storms rip through life, just remember the wind. Nothing can stop it, and no one in its path is exempt from the turmoil, chaos, and devastation that remains. Nonetheless, it does not last forever and, sure enough, make no dismay, as the sun will shine again and send the wind on its way.

When the wind knocks you over or destroys life along the way, lean on each other and build again.

Grateful Lessons

The lessons that we learn in our stumbles through life
are the ones that we need to celebrate
on the other side.

Today's pain and blistering rain
will strengthen our resolve,
as each link of the chain
fortifies the connection,
while collapsing earthly misery and disdain.

Holding On

In the
darkness,
where I
question
my life
of loss
and sin is where the knife
cuts sharpest. I contemplate
ending the awareness of great
loss, and then He gently steps in
to remind
me that
my eternal
life with
Him will
be much
greater
— not
worth
any
knick
of my
skin.

Shattered Glass

The moment in life
when our vision of the world crumbles
is like hearing shattered glass.

The moment in life
when our vision of the world crumbles
is like hearing fingernails slide across the chalkboard.

The moment in life
when our vision of the world crumbles
is like hearing soft sobs at your neighbor's funeral.

The moment in life
when our vision of the world crumbles
is like hearing someone say, "I only like you as a friend."

The moment in life
when our vision of the world crumbles
is like hearing him say, "I'm leaving you for her."

The moment in life
when our vision of the world crumbles
is like hearing the doctor say, "You don't have long."

The moment in life
when our vision of the world crumbles
is like hearing them say, "I wish you weren't born."

The moment in life

when our vision of the world crumbles
is like hearing the manager say, "Pack your desk and be
gone."

The moment in life
when our vision of the world crumbles
is like hearing your child say, "I hate you, mom."

The moment in life
when our vision of the world crumbles
is like hearing the devil say, "You're not enough. End it."

The moment in life
when our vision of the world renews
is like hearing God say, "Bless you, child, I've got you!"

Intersection of Mortality

She was falling, and all she could think of was how miserable she had lived. Her life seemed like such a waste of precious time now that the final seconds had arrived.

Tick tock, tick tock — she could feel each moment as it passed. Why is it that when living life day to day, one never truly appreciates the little things? Why does the excitement of childhood seem to diminish slowly the older one becomes, yet one day you wake up, and full-blown adulthood is the result?

Add a few runny-nosed kids, a husband that sits on the sofa each day after work while glued to the television and drinking a beer, and well, that was her life. It wasn't the one she had chosen, but the one in which she had learned to simply exist.

Every morning she awoke to the sound of screaming and crying children, shouting siblings, and barking dogs. She would slither out of bed while begging for the day to hurriedly pass because all she could think of was going back to bed to end the despair.

She needed a new life. She wanted a break. She couldn't imagine doing the same mundane run-down schedule she had done day after day, again and again.

Jumping over the edge of the rocky, hillside cliff into the cold, ominous Pacific Ocean seemed to be the only alternative. The television stations and social media outlets would pity her story and glamorize her actions for ratings. She didn't want pity. She didn't want to be the talk of the town. She didn't want to be noticed. She simply wanted to just disappear. *But how?* She had asked herself, longing for a solution.

Her body began slowly floating through the air as time stood still. She was trapped in a vortex with the final destination somewhere unknown. Her husband was sitting on the familiar sofa after work with his head hung in his hands, weeping while tears streamed down his face. Somehow, after all the years of endless name-calling, fights, and hate, he still seemed to care. She couldn't believe her eyes. All he had to do was share a word of kindness every now and then, and she wouldn't have jumped. It pained her to see him cry.

She saw her two children, ages twelve and ten, on their knees in the kitchen as police officers tried to calm the message; their mother had been in a terrible accident, and she was never coming home. Her heart literally broke in mid-air. It broke into a million pieces. Those were her precious babies. She had birthed them and loved them since the moment they took their first breath. How could she have done this to them? She knew their lives would never be the same.

She saw her dogs; they were no longer incessantly barking, and they were starving. She saw the sadness in their pitiful eyes as they realized something at home was very, very wrong. Where was mommy? She was always home, but with all this sorrow around, they couldn't comprehend.

Gasping for air, she sat up in bed, thoroughly drenched in sweat. As her eyes began to focus, relief flooded her body. It was just a bad dream, and tomorrow was a new day — in more ways than one.

Believe

- dreams come true each day

  - keep your heart honest and light

    - tomorrow begins anew

Endless Grace

Torn and shattered
beyond human repair,
I begged my Lord
to take my last breath,
as the hurt in my soul
seemed unable to rest.
When there was nothing left
but gut-wrenching shame,
my Lord turned on the light,
and I buried my face,
as His love engulfed me,
creating endless grace.

Amen.

Rainbow Tears

No matter how

long the rain

falls from the

sky,

God meets the

challenge in

reminding life

how beautiful

the journey

continues with

each teardrop

of pain,

for God's arms

wrap around us

as the hurt

tries to escape.

When the rain begins

to pass,

the reminder of His love

will shine brightly

above

in the colors of life

bent to form

a bow,

beautiful as always,

God's rainbow.

Sweet Bluebird

Bluebird
    high in the tree
        singing so softly sweet,
            reminding us of
                nature's harmony —
                    a gift from the truly
                        divine.

Merciful Love

We may not know

the why behind

His will,

but we always know

He will reveal

mercy and grace

when we need it

the most.

Persuasion

in the garden of Eden,

is where it began —

persuasion of

the tongue,

convincing

men and women

of

their desire

to

live

in

sin,

sewing clothing

to

cover the

nakedness

of their

knowledge,

hiding deep

in the

bushes

as

God walked

through

paradise.

ever since then,

humankind

has paid

for

the sins

of

one man

and

one woman,

inflicted by

the venom

of

snakeskin.

the cycle

continues

to spin

as

year after year

the

distance grows

between

the

innocence once

found

in

the

garden of life,

a stone's throw

from

the evil

and

vile

in

this

world

we now reside,

yet hope

begins

to

grow

in the seedlings

of life

that one

day,

again,

faith will

supersede

the fruit

of

our demise

— persuasion.

God's Teachings

without the burning pain

without the cold rain

without the agony of loss

without the sense of failure

love beyond the grave,

a mystery would remain.

The Downward Spiral

When you reach the bottom step,

and the earthly walls begin to close,

remember even the darkest one of all

once had wings.

Brush off the cruel shame

that the evil one brings,

turn on the light

and take a deep breath,

while He

welcomes you home.

Remembrance of Him

You are never alone,

even in the absence of another soul.

When stillness fills the air,

and the deafening sounds of despair sing,

remember inside of you,

lives the Holy King.

A Mother's Prayer

Every morning I sit and pray

for your health and safety each day.

From the moment I held you,

you took my breath away.

May God protect you every morning, noon, and night

from this evil realm that we know as life.

Holding you is like holding a piece of me,

bless your little soul, just waiting for the world to see.

Knowing you, my sweet honeybee,

is like kissing the face of God as sweetly as can be.

Every night I sit and pray,

thank you, Jesus, for another day.

Old Bones

In every pair of eyes

one can view the soul,

while some question

its existence

beyond the earthly show.

When the lights go out

and it seems no one is home,

the soul has journeyed,

leaving nothing but

brittle bones.

Shedding Guilt

Discarded remorse

and hidden pain

fall to the ground,

as shackles of guilt

and shame

dissolve

when we seek

His holy name.

The Devil's Surprise

He took everything away from her
that he could possibly think of:
food, clothing, shelter, and love.
He wallowed in smugness,
hearing each salty tear
as it gently landed, leaving her
exhausted without sleep.
He prided himself on the pain inflicted,
for destroying her life was all that he wished
because with each crashing moment,
it brought her closer to death.
He turned up the heat just a little
to enhance the process of
another human taking the fall
from God's mercy and grace,
trading it in for an eternal life of sin.
He cackled and paced
the ground beneath his horned head,
waiting for the ecstatic moment,
she would pledge a life with him,
one built on anger, hate, and division.

His blood began to boil

when his ears heard the words

"Forgive me, Dear Lord, for I have sinned. You see,

    although my life is in turmoil, and I'm hungry, again,

    I have faith you will provide me with all that I need."

Crushed and angered beyond belief, the devil packed his

bags and quietly began to leave,

for her faith must have been the size of a mustard seed,

and with patience and focus,

she truly believed

the God of man

would

win.

The Test

The purpose behind our being

is the driving force of life

beyond the immediate question

of how to survive.

Understanding the why

behind each moment of the day,

provides the fuel in forever,

keeping us focused

and on our way

to unity and togetherness,

building a bond among consciousness

that will surely withstand

the test of earthly time,

a decaying notion — at best.

Introspection

Sense of self

found in

desperation

of blending

leads to

dulled vision.

Celebrate

your uniqueness

in everything

that

you do.

Diversity

transforms

vanilla lives

to

form

myriads of color

in the

artist's tapestry

of life.

Acceptance of

others through

inclusive

domains

will lead

to

homes

worthy of

thrones.

For God

made us all

to fulfill

a

divine masterpiece.

Love one

another,

rise above,

don't fail,

and He

will take

care of

the rest

of it all.

Conundrums

Through the lens

of a microscope

life seems so unique,

yet through the lens

of the streets

life appears so bleak.

Trapped in a system

that doesn't

allow learning and growth

isn't there a way

for

God's children

to have both?

The cycle

of violence

seems to breed

greed,

while the cycle

of unity

seems to bleed

drops of humanity's

tears,

drowning out the

cries and

cheers

of the

empowered class.

With two percent

governing

all of

God's

creation,

it seems

unfathomable

those in charge

would rather see

survival dwindling

in

dilapidated

communities

of this great nation.

Yet, there are many

among us

who surely

survive

on the

death and destruction

that continues

to arise

among

the sisters and brothers

in a sea of

chaos,

turning the colors

of skin

into

a reason for fighting

within.

Until we join hands

and

smother such

calculated manipulation,

the sanctity

of living continuously yearns

for equality

of life

and the God-given

freedom

of

togetherness without strife.

Rhetorical Division

When rhetoric is used

to further the bad news,

we all take part

in embracing their twisted views.

Violence and hatred are spread

as a contagious disease that consumes,

leaving many of God's children

broken and confused.

Eliciting reaction to views on the tube

is just what the producer wanted to assimilate the mood,

as depictions of bloodshed

will eventually embed

a belief system so effective that

brotherhood will succumb to the deception.

Turn off the media and look the other way,

for love is abound and surrounds you every day.

Look for evidence in your community

of compassion

and pray

that one day conscious humanity

will flourish

and

become

mainstay.

It's a Colorful World

If only everyone could see the world through the eyes of a child, she thought.

Being a Kindergarten teacher had taught her to view life through feelings and emotions, not just words.

The sun was peeking through the bedroom window, and a smile spread across her face as the gentle reminder of love danced across the horizon.

The horror she had witnessed on the television last night before bed caused a sleepless night of tossing and turning.

Blood had been shed, lives shattered, families were being torn apart, violence and mayhem littered the city streets while the remnants of hatred shone through.

Little did the world know, by learning and embracing the symbolism of a rainbow, all lives would be enriched.

She dressed for work and began the short walk to where all the little people would be gathering in the next half hour. This gave her just enough time to prepare.

Before long, the students had all arrived, and the mood was somber.

On the chalkboard, she wrote the word RAINBOW.

Students quickly pulled out paper and crayons while they began drawing and writing words that came to mind when they visualized a rainbow.

As each student completed the assignment and presented it to the class, the heaviness in the room began to lift. Each child was able to express emotions and feelings through art.

Knowing she had given them what they needed most at the moment, she smiled and turned to write her interpretation of the colorful symbol of love.

She wrote:

Red = Love — give it; accept it; be IT.

Orange = Warmth and comfort — be kind to others.

Yellow = Happiness — the sun and flowers; dare to brighten someone's day.

Green = Renewal, earthbound, and rooted — Plant seeds for tomorrow and be thankful for mother earth.

Blue = Courage — you are all brave; be unique; be you.

Indigo = Strength — everything you need to be successful in life can be found from within. You are STRONG!

Violet = Diversity — Love it; embrace it; realize how bland life would be if everything were the same

COLOR.

Humanity's Salvation

Our nation seems so astray,
as voices scream out at night
in bloodshed and dismay
for someone else's right.

Gone are the days of light-hearted fun,
twirling and dancing had just begun.
Unbeknownst to his victims,
he sat cleaning his guns.

What in the world could they have possibly done
to deserve such a massacre from any such one?
They had never met such a despicable one,
yet he counts their last breaths, one by one.

Condemning their lifestyle was one of his last shows.
Who else could he blame for this miserable life he chose,
while others succumbed to
poverty, racism, neglect, and otherworldly woes.

For created, we did, of tomorrow's hidden hope.

The sun will again shine, and who knows?

Maybe, just maybe, humanity will grow.

The solution evades us from morning till night,

while we sit and we pray, there will be no more delight

in the cries of our friends and neighbors,

as they lose the unfair fight.

For our children are dying, and there seems no end,

but political fanatics on each extreme win.

The answer must lie somewhere in the shadows,

hidden within the hate in over-grown meadows.

The media, the news, and the shows

like to portray what they think we don't know.

When ultimately, evil blossoms

as innocently as a soft primrose.

What would happen if we all dropped to our knees,

promised to forgive and never to inflict

others in life with the same pain that we live.

Learning to love from within

is the secret we may find,

as we are all made from the same kind.

Yet divide and conquer we have been told,

let's all get together and be bold.

Fight our battles side by side,

forgoing the will to injure others over pride.

Together as a nation, we can rise above all,

but together, we must remain, once and for all.

Say no to the press, say no to the sin,

say no to the demons that crawl up from deep within.

Embrace the light of our future, together as a team,

and never again will they have the chance to demean.

No more will a mother bury her child

for something so trivial as their chosen lifestyle.

The holy one judges; it is not our part.

Love and togetherness are what we are taught.

From this moment forward, let our weapons fall down.

Hug each other for compassion has been found.

The white dove soars as the olive branch descends.

Heaven and earth will one day join again.

For, I love you, my friend

together, we are one.

All skin colors unite,

for the battle must be won.

As the sun sets on disaster and triumph begins,

our nation joins hands, and we ALL dance again.

Brotherhood stands against the veil of deceit, as when

the sun rises and sets, the dream will be complete.

Division Within

Any athletic coach will tell you that synergy is a real thing,

and it must be present amongst the players of the game

to increase the odds of a win.

Each player has a uniqueness, a difference if you will,

that collectively raises the

team's overall skill.

Joining forces in pursuit of a common goal will truly enhance

the effectiveness of any mission;

it's more than just chance.

Pay attention to the turmoil that surrounds

us these dark days,

for the division within our nation has exponentially grown,

stemming,

somehow,

from the players that know.

Part II:

Loss:

infant, father, and loved ones

Earthly Mommy

Shed no more tears,

earthly mommy of mine,

as forever entangled

is your heart and mine.

Sweet Jesus called my name,

and I couldn't resist

heaven's welcoming,

melodious tunes,

singing with such bliss.

Close your eyes,

my mommy,

and each time

that you pray,

you will feel my subtle kisses

softly dance upon your

face.

Baby Footprints

With each passing day,

I will constantly pray

that the experience of loving

me

was worth

every second of

grief.

I'm so sorry

our first meeting

was way too brief,

but remember,

no matter how much it hurts,

God's mercy and grace

will help soothe the pain.

The Lord has a way

of making each heartbeat and breath

that we take

purposefully made,

preparing us for life

beyond superficial graves.

My baby footprints on your soul

create an unending connection

mistaken — not once,

yet never forgotten,

as each tiny little toe

will continue to grow,

leaving a bond unbroken

and interwoven between

our souls.

Unending Love

Such warmth

and comfort

you have

given me,

as my life

slowly began,

so gently —

you see?

My arrival

may not have

gone

as carefully planned,

but the love between us

will never

end.

Baby Angel

God spoke to me

in the womb

and explained how He

needed me most,

as my angel wings

were already grown.

Please don't be sad,

as death only occurs on earth,

for the soul will emerge

victorious in grace,

and tailored angel wings

will descend from

heavenly

origin.

Mother and Child

Love,

above all,

transforms each moment

of our

destiny.

Once we love

each other,

nothing can erase,

the magic that occurs

between mother and child,

so regardless of how difficult

the moment seems to be,

remember love

such as this

will

                           never cease.

Guardian Angel

We will meet again

in tomorrow's delight,

but until then,

Mommy and Daddy,

never lose sight

of my presence

that will fill your heart,

night after night.

Lucid Laughs

The anguish that grips me from that

horrific day

chokes me most

when I

lie down

to sleep.

As I close my eyes,

it wells up

within,

reminding me of how

much you

needlessly suffered,

begging

to be

born

again.

I learned

that day

that

a connection exists,

energy amongst

souls

that

science can't

resist,

for

I awoke just as

you

were leaving

this world

to sit

among the angels

that

watch over

this wretched earth.

My saving

grace

is the

time that we shared

downstairs

in my media room,

laughing again.

You looked so

peaceful,

happy,

while you grinned,

and we

reminisced

as though

the cancer

had never been.

You were so at

ease,

and

your gift of peace

is a blanket

that covers me

when my heart

begins

to ache

and

misery

is then released.

Thank you,

dear dad,

for all the lessons

that

you taught,

for the bravery

you showed me

when

you weathered

the

demons of this life,

only to show

the world

how glorious it will be

in the afterlife.

These lucid laughs

that

we share

together

will always remain

memories,

occurring

beyond the grave.

For those that don't

believe,

let's show them

they are wrong,

for the mind

remembers

the difference

in the presence

of a heavenly soul.

The dream visitation

is much more

sincere

without a worry

in sight

because when we leave this earth

we will surely find

the eternal

bliss that only God can provide.

Sharing with others

is

a task that

one

must engage

when they

leave

this side

for

eternal embrace.

Spiritual Seed

Missing someone

is a heartache

that consumes the soul.

I have planted tiny seeds inside of you

that will grow

if you gently water

them and encourage them to

take hold.

A part of me

will forever be rooted in us.

Take a chance and believe,

for God

promised

that faith

leads to eternity.

Forever Father

Strong advice he gave
when he knew she needed it most.
Father from the grave.

A Baby's Prayer

Some things in life
just don't make sense.
Trying as we must
to wade through the muck,
leads to moments of
desperate need.
Don't close the door
to compassion as others try to help,
for God gave us each other
to embrace our humanness
through life's most challenging moments.
Through great pain
manifests spiritual growth.
Give God the chance to heal your pain,
for together with Him
we must all remain
to meet again,
while angels sing songs
of glorious ever-after.

Follow my lead and
leave fear behind
because when the journey is over,
the only thing that will have mattered
are the connections we made
through everlasting love.

Warm Thoughts

His wings

came much too soon

              so many memories

              sleep warmly beside me each night

miss you

My Wish

It began many years ago. You were my mentor, my savior, my one true person in life that touched my soul like no other. It was the little things like learning to tie a shoelace, walking to the corner drugstore for stick candy, and holding me tight on the twister rides at the local carnival.

My first boyfriend — my first breakup — you kissed the tears away as your heart tore into two while telling me you had seen him being unfaithful from afar.

The torment in your eyes when our family dog had to be put down after many years of backyard fetch — the pride in your face as you escorted me across the gymnasium floor for my senior homecoming court.

It was holding my arm as I walked down the aisle to say 'I do' to the man of my dreams, while my legs were so shaky, I could barely stand.

The joy on your face the day I told you another little girl was going to steal your heart, and yes, she did. Holding that first baby grandchild bundle must have grown your heart tenfold. I named her after you because it was one of those special gifts that bring meaning to life — one that couldn't be bought.

Love is a complex word, and it conveys many emotions. Some picture red hearts, cupids, and long stem roses. Some picture romantic tropical destinations for two. I picture you; everything about you.

You taught me that no matter how hard it gets, no matter how ugly the situation is, no matter how heart-wrenching it can be, one can find strength from within.

Our journey of loss began a few years before that fateful day. Your strength, tenacity, and endurance were something to marvel. Many times, you were consoling me without even knowing. You thought I was strong, but I was oh so weak.

The tears, the desperate prayers, the hidden hurt that took place on my pillow every night was something I just couldn't let you see.

Cancer wouldn't get the chance to take that from me.

As I sat beside you those last few days, we joked, laughed, prayed, and we knew our time was very short. I wanted to run because the pain was so intense — at times, I couldn't breathe.

But I stayed because I remember all of the love and strength you had given me. I begged you to let me know when you reached "the other side." I told you I couldn't go on in life without a sign that you had safely arrived.

My WISH, my one lasting hope, was that you would find peace. My WISH came true.

Your love surpasses time and space, and your presence is felt daily from the visiting bluebirds to the butterflies and the blooming azalea garden you had planted mysteriously on the first anniversary of your death.

Love transcends the grave; life is eternal, and you are in a special place.

I love you, dad.

Broken Mortality

Inside of your heart

lives the mortal manifestation

of love.

The earthly spirit is grounded

by human essence abound.

When it comes time to leave this earth,

spiritual light transforms the confound

of artificial walls,

escaping earthly boundaries,

while making its presence known.

The remainder that lives in the heart

transcends to create an unending connection

between Father and child.

Without you,

I would never have known

blind love and pure faith.

Sweet Confessions

Each heart has a distinct beat, just like each snowflake is so unique.

I heard yours from the inside, as it always comforted me.

I will always love you, earthly mommy.

Homeward Bound

God gives us time with His children as He needs.

Our roles as parents are to watch over and love them as one
of our own,

but ultimately, remembering,

they are only on loan.

His timing may be confusing but never forget that

God's masterplan is much greater

than any will of our own.

In sorrowful times, such as a young child going home,

lean on your Father,

for peace is found within the great

"I am."

Divine Parents

Once you conceive a child,

forever after will be known,

as the divide between heaven and earth

disintegrates

when we journey home.

Earthly parents and children will walk heaven's sidewalks

as eternally-bound souls.

Whispers of Life

The lessons we learn by leaning in

are the challenges we must face

for life ever after

with Him.

Each pair of angel wings

are hand-sewn from above,

as God gently whispers

life

into each body and soul.

Some are so special

they don't live on earth long,

for our Father in heaven

truly knows

what resides inside

just itching

to grow,

so the wings of a child spread open,

soaring high above,

leaving loved ones below.

Peaceful Goodbyes

Watching and waiting,

while his chest rises and falls

with each earthly breath,

paralyzing my thoughts of the pain that I will gain

when the last ounce of oxygen

enters his brain.

My life without him

is dreadful at best,

and the agony of losing him

is the cause of my deep unrest.

Then it happens with such sudden finesse,

the soul leaves the body,

as his face gently falls,

replacing earthly color in his cheeks

with the grayness of defeat,

yet the transcendence of life

is now

complete.

Dear Daddy

As you lay sleeping

I sit here and mourn.

That dreadful day dreaming,

the nightmare of you leaving.

The grim reaper lies in wait,

as your labored breath seems to hesitate.

My life flashes before me

as childhood memories play,

somehow, there just has to be a better way.

I see your pain and suffering clearly,

Oh, how I wish I could ease the weary.

As your life begins to transform with time,

your face displays conflict, as well as mine.

As you are torn between heaven and here,

wanting the sickness to end,

but missing your loved ones, I fear.

To the bitter end,

I hold your hand and softly pray

for God to help you as true love stays

forever in our hearts and treasured in our souls.

Cancer won't win because no matter where you are,

in this world or His, we shall never be apart.

Some things are better left unspoken,

like the soft, gentle wind

that lifts the spirit lightly so your new tomorrow can begin.

As you leave mother earth

the angels sing of praise,

for another one of God's children

has journeyed a long way.

The love of father and child will carry us through,

as I learn to live my life without you.

I planted your azalea garden,

and I can feel you near

as I sit and ponder your life up there.

I hung the bluebird house where you told me to,

and I visit with you often

with each little birdie that is anew.

One day I will see you

and hug you again.

But for now, dear daddy,

I love and miss you till then.

Stillborn

You took my

soul when you left

without a

proper

goodbye.

Now, I must

live my life

only

partially whole,

broken into pieces,

fractured and weak.

End of Life

The cycle of life

is difficult to understand,

for as humanity ages

awareness akin

to mature souls

emerges from within,

and the opportunities

of earthly life

begin to sink in,

and the sadness of wasted experiences

gradually bubbles up,

trying to steal your joy

with rememberings of

lost moments, again.

Regardless of the turmoil

that seems to never end,

embrace each moment

of this life,

reminiscing the gift.

Without defining moments

of trials and thoughts of sin,

the soul would not graduate

into everlasting

bliss in

living with Him.

Humbling Creed

In the aftermath of despair, there is a stillness that overcomes the air. Quiet moments of silent reflection make one painfully aware of the absence of a loved one that is no longer there. These moments of grief can be overwhelming, and the question seeps in. Why did this happen, and how am I to begin again?

This is where faith steps in and the reminder of how a mustard seed can manifest the strength to move mountains — with Him. Love has a way of releasing anger harvested deep within, but the choice must be made to blindly follow His lead.

Humanity was created as an extension of God's grace. The designer has already contemplated each and every day. Life events don't define us, for His mercy is great, and all we must do is simply embrace the idea that through Him, all things are made.

Night Sky

Gazing at the night sky in wonder and disbelief,

he couldn't help but wonder

if it could possibly be

his newborn son, sleeping softly up yonder,

unaware below of the treacherous storm of grief.

For a parent to lose a child just didn't seem right;

all the planning and excitement around such a sweet

surprise, left the new father overwhelmed

in the presence of such horrific disappointment.

With unanswered questions and jagged scars, he violently

wept for his son in the stars.

As the pain became unbearable, a miracle occurred, and a

tap on his shoulder shook him alert.

There was no one there when he lifted his head, yet the

ambiance he felt seemed so surreal, followed by a peace that

revealed a calmness of the sea.

A smile crossed his face when he realized

at once, his son was not only okay but was

safely nestled in the stars above.

Hidden Predator

The anger that surrounded me
encapsulated my every thought.

The horror, the harm, the fight till death
seemed unnecessary and senseless from the start.

The days turned into weeks,
and before long, the seasons passed.

Each month was another reminder about the
end approaching fast.

The heart knows no method
of suppressing the worry,
as to our loved ones, we are connected
through every fiber in a fury.

Like an unseen threat
hidden deep inside,

cancer preys and invades

mortal bodies in a tragic

game

of charades.

Disguised from the world,

the intrinsic battleground

is a constant reminder

of the perversity that kills from within.

Could it be unkinder?

Brotherly Love

Dark forces inside my head,

beg me to embrace,

misery and dread.

Anxiety and depression,

are my new best friends,

since you've been gone.

How long has it been?

Evil lurks in the shadows,

preying on the broken,

waiting to steal,

yet never once awoken.

Hell is real,

it's a place you can visit,

the mystery of unhappiness,

swipes the soul's only meal.

Raise the blinds to your heart,

let the light shine within,

as trusting my brain,

has been the only sin.

Tomorrow lives on,

clean the cobwebs above,

forgive and forget,

in the name of brotherly love.

Accident

Soft whispers in the breeze.

I long for thee.

Your voice in my head —

how I live with such dread.

Missing you

is like missing part of me.

Forever apart,

I still can't believe.

They say wrong place,

wrong time,

but it is beyond me,

why heaven took you,

and left me here without

"we."

Without You

Without you,

I would have never known me.

Without you,

I would have never known love beyond boundaries.

Without you,

I would have never understood the essence of human compassion.

Without you,

I would have never looked inside of me.

Without you,

I would have never experienced a love kinder than a physical connection.

Without you,

I would have never experienced a loss so great that even words can not fathom.

Without you,

I would have never known what it is like to truly miss someone.

Thank you for loving and leaving me.

Author News

M. Gail Grant would like to thank her readers and kindly ask you to leave a review on GoodReads and the vendor from which you purchased your book if you feel inclined to do so! She is very grateful for your feedback and thoughts for future readers.

Join our mailing list to receive periodic updates on new releases, sale information, and local author events:

MGailGrant.com
Facebook.com/MGailGrant
Twitter.com/MGailGrant
Instagram.com/MGailGrant

Other Reads

by
M. Gail Grant:

Poetry:

Bluebirds and Faith

Faith-Based Fantasy Fiction
Middle-Grade Series:

Magdalena Gottschalk: The Crooked Trail

Magdalena Gottschalk: The Slippery Slope

Magdalena Gottschalk: Lindtzl Kingdom

Magdalena Gottschalk: The Grand Ball ... *Coming Soon*